Introduction

Welcome to the wonderful world of Hot Air

"What is Hot Air Frying?" I hear you say.
It is simply using Hot Air to cook the food. An ingenious and easy method of cooking which is not just about frying, as you will see from the wide variety of recipes in this book.

The Hot air fryer is an invaluable and versatile piece of kitchen equipment enabling you to prepare quick and delicious meals as well as tasty homemade chips.

As your hot air fryer needs only a small amount of oil to work its magic, you may use your favourite quality oil such as olive oil.

This book contains a selection of my recipe creations which have been tried and tested on a range of Hot air fryers to ensure that all recipes are successful.

I love experimenting in the kitchen and would encourage you to do the same. You can adapt the recipes by adding or changing ingredients according to your own taste. Have fun creating!

Appliance Guide

Important! Please Read....

Please note, I mention the temperatures to use in my recipes, If your Hot air fryer has a pre-set temperature of around 170°c , then disregard these.

Some fryers use a pan with a paddle that you put your food directly in and some are like mini ovens that you place the food in an oven safe dish or on a rack, please always use your air fryer following manufacturers instructions.

Some Hot air fryers require pre-heating. If this is the case with yours, ensure you do this first. If not, simply follow the recipe.

Does your Hot air fryer automatically stir your food? If not, you need to manually stir the food occasionally during cooking. Always stir with a wooden or plastic utensil to prevent damage to the non-stick surface.

Always follow the manufacturer's instructions. Always place the food in the correct cooking pan or suitable dish in accordance with the manufacturer's instructions. Never leave your appliance unattended.

Follow correct cooking procedures....

When adding dried herbs or seasoning, always ensure you mix them with a liquid, such as oil.

All temperatures, times and instructions are given as a guide only and should always be adjusted accordingly at the time of cooking.

Contents / Index

Top Tip!... The bacon & croutons make a tasty topping for soups.

Bacon & Crouton Salad

Ingredients
Serves 2-3

Croutons
2 slices thick granary bread
¼ tsp garlic salt
1½ tbsp olive oil
¼ tsp mixed herbs
½ tbsp apricot jam mixed with
　　½ tbsp boiling water.
4 rashers streaky bacon
　　(chopped)

Dressing
1 tsp mustard
2 tbsp olive oil
1 tbsp vinegar
Pinch salt & pepper

Method
1. Put the olive oil, apricot jam, mixed herbs and garlic salt in a bowl. Mix to a paste.
2. Remove crusts off the granary bread and cut into 1cm cubes.
3. Add the cubed bread and chopped bacon to the bowl and mix.
4. Set the hot air fryer to 170°c (if applicable). Place the mixture in the hot air fryer pan or basket and cook for 6-8 minutes or until cooked.
5. For the dressing, mix the mustard, olive oil, vinegar, salt & pepper together.

Serve over a mixed salad.

Top Tip!... Add chorizo sausage for a spicy flavour, this will also make the prawns go further.

Garlic Prawns

Ingredients   **Serves 3 - 4**

350g prawns (peeled, tails on)
2 cloves garlic (peeled & finely
   chopped)
Pinch salt & pepper
25g butter (soft)
1 tbsp sweet chilli sauce
1 Lemon (quartered)
1 tbsp sweet sherry
Garnish
1 tbsp parsley (optional)

Method

1. Put the prawns, garlic, butter, sweet chilli sauce, sherry, lemon, salt and pepper in a bowl and mix.
2. Set the hot air fryer to 170°c (if applicable). Pour into a suitable dish and place in a hot air fryer basket or directly into the hot air fryer pan, and cook for 10 minutes or until thoroughly cooked.
3. Best served immediately, (piping hot), garnish with parsley.

Serve with salad and crusty bread to dip in the sauce.

9

Top Tip!... You can always change the seasoning
e.g. curry powder & paprika .

Wedges

Ingredients   **Serves 4**

Wedges
4 medium potatoes
1 tsp jerk seasoning
1 tbsp mango chutney
½ tsp garlic salt
1 tbsp mayonnaise (full fat)
Dip
50ml sour cream
1 tsp chopped chives

Method

1. Cut the potatoes into wedges.
2. Put the wedges, jerk seasoning, mango chutney, mayonnaise and garlic salt in a bowl and mix.
3. Set the hot air fryer to 170°c (if applicable). Pour into a suitable dish and place in a hot air fryer basket or directly into the hot air fryer pan and cook for 25 minutes or until thoroughly cooked.
4. To make the dip, mix sour cream with the chives and serve.

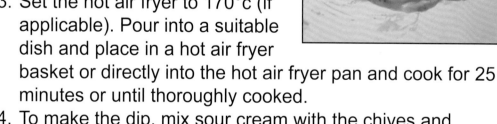

Serve with sour cream and chives dip.

Top Tip!... You can use monkfish instead of scallops and streaky bacon instead of pancetta.

Scallops Wrapped in Pancetta

Ingredients   **Makes 8**

8 scallops
8 pancetta (slices)
4 sage leaves
8 cocktail sticks
Pinch white pepper
1 tsp olive oil
Garnish:
Lemon wedges

Method

1. Sprinkle the scallops with white pepper. Wrap with ½ piece of sage and sliced pancetta.
2. Secure with a cocktail stick.
3. Rub the wrapped scallops with the olive oil.
4. Set the hot air fryer to 170°c (if applicable). Put the scallops in the hot air fryer pan or basket and cook for 6-10 minutes depending on your preference.

Serve with mixed leaf salad, lemon wedges and cherry tomatoes.

Top Tip!... Use shoulder of lamb as an alternative to duck and instead of pancakes wrap the duck in lettuce leaves.

Shredded Duck for Pancake Rolls

Ingredients

Serves 4-5

2 duck legs
3 tbsp soy sauce
2 tbsp hoisin sauce
½ tbsp salt

Serve with:
15 Chinese style pancakes
4 tbsp plum sauce
2 tbsp hoisin sauce
½ cucumber (peeled & cut into
   strips)
6 spring onions (cut into strips)
2 little gem lettuces (optional)

Method

1. Put the duck legs in a pan and cover with boiling water.
2. Add 2 tbsp hoisin sauce and 2 tbsp soy sauce, boil for 45 minutes.
3. Remove the duck legs from the pan and dry with paper towel.
4. Score the duck skin, rub with the salt and coat with 1 tbsp soy sauce.
5. Set the hot air fryer to 170°c (if applicable). Place the legs in the hot air fryer pan or basket and cook for 15-20 minutes until golden brown.
6. Shred using a fork.

Serve in pancakes with a mixture of plum and hoisin sauce, mixed cucumber and spring onion. (If you want to make hoisin sauce similar to the one you get with crispy duck from the takeaway, mix in a little golden syrup.

15

Top Tip!... Use mozzarella cheese instead of pâté.

Stuffed Mushrooms

Ingredients   **Makes 9**

9 closed cup mushrooms
½ tsp olive oil
50g pâté
9 rashers streaky bacon
9 leaves basil
9 cocktail sticks
Garnish:
Mixed leaves
Garlic Mayonnaise

Method

1. Clean and de-stalk the mushrooms, fill the centre of the mushrooms with the pâté and top with a basil leaf.
2. Wrap the mushroom, with streaky bacon and secure with a cocktail stick. Rub with oil.
3. Set the hot air fryer to 170°c (if applicable). Place the mushrooms in the hot air fryer pan or basket and cook for 10 minutes or until thoroughly cooked.

Serve with a green salad and garlic mayonnaise.

Top Tip!... Great to take on picnics. Add some mango chutney to the curry paste to create a less fiery dish. Can also be made using red Thai curry paste.

Thai Green Curry Wings

Ingredients   **Serves 3**

500g chicken wings
1 tbsp Thai green curry paste
½ tbsp sesame oil
1 tbsp mayonnaise
Garnish:
Spring Onions
Red Peppers
Sliced Carrot

Method

1. Mix the chicken wings, sesame oil, Thai green curry paste and mayonnaise, in a bowl.
2. Set the hot air fryer to 170°c (if applicable). Pour into a suitable dish and place in a hot air fryer basket or directly into the hot air fryer pan, and cook for 15 - 20 minutes or until thoroughly cooked.

Serve with mixed salad leaves or as a main course with rice.

Top Tip!... Be adventurous, try butternut squash
or sweet potato as alternatives.

Vegetable Medley

Ingredients   **Serves 4**

1 large potato (peeled)
¼ tbsp oil
1 tbsp mayonnaise (full fat)
Pinch salt & pepper
1 tsp paprika
2 sprigs rosemary (picked)
 1 clove garlic (chopped)
¼ medium swede or turnip
  (peeled)
1 small parsnip (peeled)
1 medium beetroot (peeled)
1 carrot (peeled)
½ onion

Method

1. Chop the potato, Swede, parsnip, beetroot, carrot and onion into cubes and put into a bowl. Add oil and mayonnaise, paprika, garlic, rosemary, salt & pepper and mix.

2. Set the hot air fryer to 170°c (if applicable) Place into the hot air fryer pan or basket. Cook for 20-30 minutes or until thoroughly cooked. Stir occasionally if required.

Serve with roast or grilled meat and steamed vegetables.

Top Tip!... You can use chestnut mushrooms
instead of the beef.

Beef Stroganoff

Ingredients
Serves 2

250g beef (strips fillet or sirloin)
1 yellow pepper
   (Deseeded & sliced)
1 garlic clove (peeled & crushed)
75ml double cream
½ medium onion (sliced)
1 tbsp olive oil
1 tsp dijon mustard
1 tsp cornflour mixed with 25ml
   water.
2 tbsp sherry (sweet or dry)
4 closed cup mushrooms (sliced)
1 chicken stock cube mixed with
   100ml boiling water.
1 tsp dark soy sauce
Pinch salt & pepper.

Method

1. Put the beef, onion, peppers, garlic, mushrooms, olive oil, salt & pepper in a bowl and mix thoroughly.
2. Set the hot air fryer to 170°c (if applicable). Pour into a suitable dish and place in a hot air fryer basket or directly into the hot air fryer pan, and cook for 10 minutes.
3. Put the mustard, cream, soy sauce, sherry, cornflour and stock together in a bowl and mix. Add to the other ingredients in the hot air fryer. Stir and cook for a further 5 minutes, or until thoroughly cooked.

Serve with rice.

Top Tip!... Makes a great pie filling! Try Using using fish and/or prawns instead of chicken & serve with mashed potato.

Chicken à la King

Ingredients   **Serves 4**

2 chicken breasts (diced)
½ onion (diced)
½ red pepper (deseeded & sliced)
½ green pepper (sliced)
1 garlic (peeled & finely chopped)
1 tbsp olive oil
Pinch salt
¼ tsp pepper
1 chicken stock cube mixed with
   250ml of boiling water.
100ml single cream
½ tbsp cornflour mixed with 25ml
   cold water.

Method

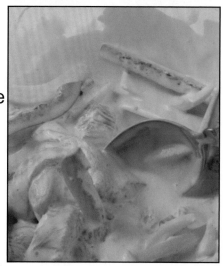

1. Put the chicken, onion, red pepper, green pepper, garlic, olive oil, salt & pepper in a bowl and mix.
2. Set the hot air fryer to 170°c (if applicable). Pour into a suitable dish and place in a hot air fryer basket or directly into the hot air fryer pan, and cook for 8 minutes.
3. Add the stock, cream, and cornflour to the hot air fryer, cook for a further 6 minutes, or until thoroughly cooked. Stir occasionally if required.

Serve with rice or over a jacket potato.

Top Tip!... Can be served cold and used as a buffet item or at a picnic. This stuffing works great with roast chicken.

Chicken Stuffed with Chorizo

Ingredients   **Makes 6**

 6 Chicken drumsticks
1 chorizo sausage
1 tsp paprika
1 tsp olive oil
Pinch salt & pepper
1 ½ tbsp sage & onion stuffing
  mix.
6 cocktail sticks

Method

1. Chop the chorizo into small pieces and put in a bowl with the paprika, sage and onion stuffing. Add a little boiling water to form a stuffing mixture. Season.

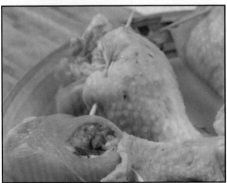

2. Make a small pocket in each of the drumsticks with a knife and fill with the stuffing. Secure with a cocktail stick and rub with oil.

3. Set the hot air fryer to 170°c (if applicable). Place in the Hot air fryer pan or basket and cook for 20 minutes or until thoroughly cooked.

Serve with mixed leaves and potato salad.

Top Tip!... This chicken with cashew nuts dish can be served separately with rice instead of mixing with noodles.

Chicken with Cashew Nuts

Ingredients   **Serves 4**

2 chicken breasts (cut in strips)
1 red pepper (sliced)
2 tbsp cashew nuts
1 tbsp dark soy sauce
4 tbsp tomato sauce
1 tsp vinegar
1 tin pineapple in juice 140g
  (cut into pieces)
1 tsp sesame seed oil
1 onions (large chunks)
1 garlic (peeled & finely chopped)
1 cm square ginger (peeled &
  finely chopped)
500g cooked egg or rice noodles
  (150g uncooked weight)

Method

1. Put the chicken, red pepper, cashew nuts, soy sauce, tomato sauce, vinegar, pineapple, sesame seed oil, onion, garlic and ginger in a large bowl and mix .
2. Set the hot air fryer to 170°c (if applicable). Pour into a suitable dish and place in a Hot air fryer basket or directly into the hot air fryer pan, and cook for 20-30 minutes or until thoroughly cooked.
3. Cook the noodles so they are ready to serve at the same time as the chicken.
4. Combine the chicken with the noodles in a large bowl using two forks.

Serve with steamed pak choi.

Top Tip!... Use fresh or tinned pineapple instead of mango.

Mango Chicken

Ingredients   **Serves 2-3**
4 chicken thighs (cut into strips)
1 tbsp jerk seasoning
60g fresh mango (diced)
1 tbsp mayonnaise
1 tbsp sweet chilli sauce
½ tsp garlic salt
Garnish
Fresh lime wedges

Method

1. Put the chicken, jerk seasoning, mango, mayonnaise, sweet chilli sauce and garlic salt in a bowl and mix.
2. Set the hot air fryer to 170°c (if applicable). Pour into a suitable dish and place in a hot air fryer basket or directly into the Hot air fryer pan, and cook for 12-15 minutes or until thoroughly cooked.

Serve with rice or in a pitta bread with salad and garnish with a wedge of lime.

Top Tip!... You can change the mixed beans to chickpeas or flageolet beans.

Mixed Bean Cassoulet

Ingredients   **Serves 2**

4 sausages (optional Toulouse)
1 duck breast (sliced)
1 tin mixed beans (420g)
1 tin chopped tomatoes (400g)
Pinch salt & pepper
½ tsp mixed herbs
1 chicken stock cube mixed with
   400ml of boiling water.
1 tbsp tomato sauce

Method

1. Set the hot air fryer to 170°c (if applicable). Place duck and sausages into a suitable dish and place in a hot air fryer basket or directly into the hot air fryer pan, and cook for 11 minutes.
2. Drain away the excess fat. Remove the sausages and slice.
3. Put mixed beans, tomatoes, mixed herbs, chicken stock, tomato sauce, salt & pepper in a bowl and mix.
4. Add the duck and sausage and stir.
5. Return to the hot air fryer pan or suitable dish and cook for a further 10 minutes or until thoroughly cooked.

Serve with crusty bread.

33

Top Tip!.. Add bean sprouts, mange tout, broccoli and baby corn to extend the recipe.

Oriental Duck

Ingredients   **Serves 2**
1 duck breast
1 tbsp honey
1 tbsp soy sauce
½ tbsp oyster sauce
½ green pepper (sliced)
½ onion (sliced)
½ tsp Chinese five spice
¼ tsp salt

Method

1. Score the duck breast and rub with salt.
2. Set the hot air fryer to 170°c (if applicable). Pour into a suitable dish and place in a hot air fryer basket or directly into the hot air fryer pan, and cook for 11 minutes.
3. Remove excess fat.
4. Remove the duck and slice.
5. Put the duck slices with honey, soy sauce, oyster sauce, green pepper, onion and five spice in a bowl and mix.
6. Return to the Hot air fryer pan or suitable dish and cook for a further 9 minutes or until thoroughly cooked.

Serve with rice or noodles.

Top Tip!...Use chicken, pork or prawns as an alternative to beef.

Steak in a Black Bean Sauce

Ingredients   **Serves 2**

1 large sirloin steak (sliced)
130g black bean sauce
½ onion (chopped)
½ red pepper (sliced)
4 chestnut mushrooms (quartered)
8 mange tout
1 tsp sesame seed oil
1 clove garlic (chopped)(optional)

Method

1. Put the sirloin steak, onion, peppers, mange tout, mushroom, garlic and sesame seed oil in a bowl and mix.
2. Set the hot air fryer to 170°c (if applicable). Pour into a suitable dish and place in a hot air fryer basket or directly into the hot air fryer pan, and cook for 9 minutes.
3. Add the black bean sauce and continue cooking for a further 6 minutes or until thoroughly cooked.
4. If the mixture has started to dry out at the end of cooking period, add 1 tbsp of water.

Serve with rice or noodles.

Top Tip!... For spicy ribs, change the sweet chilli
sauce to chilli sauce.

Sticky Pork Ribs

Ingredients — **Serves 2**

500g pork ribs
Glaze
2 tbsp apricot jam
2 cloves garlic (peeled & crushed)
¼ tsp mixed herbs
1 tbsp mayonnaise
1 tsp soy sauce

Method

1. Place the pork ribs in a pan and cover with boiling water and boil for 30 minutes.
2. Remove from the pan and dry with paper towel.
3. For the glaze, mix together the apricot jam, garlic, mixed herbs, mayonnaise and soy sauce.
4. Coat the ribs with the glaze.
5. Set the hot air fryer to 170°c (if applicable), Place in the hot air fryer pan or basket and cook for 8-10 minutes or until thoroughly cooked.

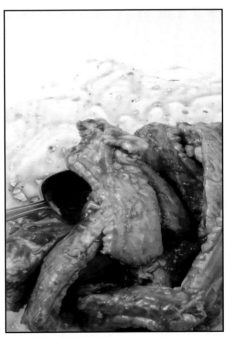

Serve with special fried rice or noodles.

Top Tip!... Use mozzarella or chilli cheese
instead of cream cheese.

Stuffed Chicken Breast

Ingredients **Serves 2**

2 chicken breasts (skin on)
1 clove garlic (peeled & chopped)
1 tbsp cream cheese
¼ red pepper
   (deseeded & chopped)
¼ red onion (finely chopped)
Pinch salt & pepper
4 cocktail sticks
¼ olive oil

Method

1. Put the red pepper, onion, cream cheese and garlic in a bowl and mix.
2. Using a knife, cut a pocket in the chicken breasts and stuff with the cream cheese mixture. Secure each breast with two cocktail sticks.
3. Rub the chicken breast with olive oil, salt & pepper.
4. Set the hot air fryer to 170°c (if applicable), Place in the hot air fryer pan or basket and cook for 15-20 minutes or until thoroughly cooked.

Serve with rice or noodles.

Top Tip!... Use ¼ tsp of cinnamon to the recipe to give it that authentic Eastern flavour.

Sweet Chilli Lamb

Ingredients   **Makes 14**

Balls
400g lamb mince
1/2 onion (finely chopped)
2 tbsp sweet chilli sauce
3 tbsp plain flour
1 small egg
1 clove garlic
   (peeled & finely chopped)
¼ tsp mixed Herbs
Pinch salt & pepper
Dip
4 tbsp sour cream
1 tbsp chopped chives
2 tbsp mayonnaise
¼ cucumber (small, diced)

Method

1. Put the lamb mince, finely chopped onion, sweet chilli sauce, flour, egg, garlic, mixed herbs, salt & pepper into a bowl and mix together.
2. Roll into 14 small balls, put onto a tray and put in the freezer for 1 hour to set.
3. Set the hot air fryer to 170°c (if applicable), put the balls in the hot air fryer pan or basket for 15-20 minutes or until thoroughly cooked.
4. Put the sour cream, chives, mayonnaise, and cucumber together and mix. Serve with the lamb.

Serve with cous cous.

43

Top Tip!...Use Chicken or prawns instead
of lamb.

Tandoori Lamb with Mint & Sour Cream Dip

Ingredients   Serves 2

Tandoori Lamb
300g leg of lamb (cubed)
½ tbsp tandoori paste or
    seasoning
1 tbsp Greek yoghurt
½ tbsp mango chutney
Pinch salt & pepper
Dip
1 sprig mint (chopped)
2 tbsp sour cream
Garnish:
½ Lemon (cut into wedges)
4 sprigs coriander

Method

1. Put the Greek yoghurt, mango chutney, tandoori seasoning, salt & pepper and mix.
   Add the cubed lamb and mix to coat.
2. Set the hot air fryer to 170°c (if applicable), Place in the
3. hot air fryer pan or basket and cook for 15-20 minutes or until thoroughly cooked.
4. For the dip, mix the sour cream and mint.

Serve with a mint and sour cream dip, naan breads,rice, lemon and corriander.

45

Top Tip!... Use the Prawns for prawn cocktail to make a delicious starter.

Tandoori Prawns

Ingredients   **Serves 3**

Tandoori Prawns
18 prawns (peeled, tails on)
1 tbsp tandoori seasoning or
   paste
1 clove garlic (peeled & crushed)
1 tbsp sweet chilli sauce
1 tbsp mayonnaise
9 cocktail sticks

Pilaf Rice
1 cup basmati rice
1 cardamom pod
¼ tsp turmeric
2 cups boiling water
5 cloves

Garnish: lemon wedges

Method

1. Put the prawns, tandoori seasoning, sweet chilli sauce, garlic and mayonnaise into a bowl and mix.
2. Place the coated prawns onto cocktail sticks, 2 prawns per stick.
3. Set the hot air fryer to 170°c (if applicable), Place in the hot air fryer pan or basket and cook for 6-10 minutes or until thoroughly cooked.
4. To make the pilaf rice put ingredients into a pan, bring to the boil, simmer for 15 minutes and serve.

Serve with pilau rice.

Top Tip!... Monkfish, Swordfish or any other firm fish can be used instead of Tuna.

Tuna Kebabs

Ingredients **Makes 14**
1 tuna steak (cut into squares)
1 red onion (cut into squares)
1 tin pineapple chunks (150g)
1 red pepper (cut into squares)
1 tbsp sweet chilli sauce
1 tbsp olive oil
Pinch salt & pepper
2 sprigs coriander
14 cocktail sticks

Method

1. Assemble the tuna, red pepper, red onion and pineapple on the cocktail sticks to make the kebabs. Season with salt and pepper.
2. Mix together the oil with the sweet chilli sauce and brush over the kebabs.
3. Set the hot air fryer to 170°c (if applicable), Place in the hot air fryer pan or basket and cook for 6-8 minutes or until thoroughly cooked.

Serve with rice and salad. Garnish with coriander.

Top Tip!... Add the berry compote to ice cream to create the ultimate topping!

Berry Compote with Meringue

Ingredients   **Serves 4**

200g mixed frozen berries
3 tbsp icing sugar
1 tbsp blackcurrant jelly
2 tbsp port
250ml double cream
3 meringue nests
Garnish:
Mint

Method

1. Put the frozen berries, icing sugar, blackcurrant jelly and port in a bowl and mix.
2. Set the Hot air fryer to 170°c (if applicable). Pour into a suitable dish and place in a hot air fryer basket or directly into the hot air fryer pan, and cook for 6-10 minutes.
3. Remove and leave to cool.
4. Whip the double cream, and break up the meringue nests into small pieces.
5. Place the meringue into serving dishes with the cream and pour cold berry mix over the top.

Serve with sprig of mint.

Top Tip!... Instead of pancakes, pour over slices of chocolate Swiss roll.

Boozy Cherry Pancakes

Ingredients   **Serves 4**

2 tbsp cherry brandy
350g fresh cherries (stones & stalks
        removed)
2 tbsp golden syrup
25g butter (melted)
1 tbsp arrowroot mixed with a little
        cold water
4 pancakes
4 scoops ice cream or whipped
cream

Method

1. Put arrowroot and cherry brandy into
   a bowl and mix. Add the cherries,
   syrup, melted butter and mix.
2. Set the hot air fryer to 170°c (if
   applicable). Pour into a suitable dish
   and place in a hot air fryer basket
   or directly into the hot air fryer pan,
   and cook for 12-15 minutes until the
   sauce starts to go translucent.
3. Remove from the hot air fryer and
   pour hot cherries over pancakes.
   Serve with whipped cream or ice cream.

It is easier to remove the stones after cooking the cherries.
We recommend that you remove the stones prior to serving.

Top Tip!...You can use prunes instead of dates and serve with waffles or pancakes instead of brioche.

Date & Banana with Toffee Sauce over Brioche

Ingredients   **Serves 4**

2 bananas (cut into 2cm chunks)
8 dates (stoned & quartered)
1 tbsp dark brown sugar
25g butter
1 tbsp honey
1 brioche or fruit loaf
1 tbsp icing sugar

Method

1. Put the banana and dates, brown sugar, honey, butter in a bowl and mix.
2. Set the hot air fryer to 170°c (if applicable). Pour into a suitable dish and place in a hot air fryer basket or directly into the hot air fryer pan, and cook for 7-10 minutes.
3. Slice the brioche and toast in a toaster.
4. Place toasted brioche on a plate and spoon over the banana and date toffee.
5. Dust with icing sugar.

Serve with ice cream.

55

Top Tip!...
    Try using apples
    instead of pears.

Honey Pears

Ingredients   **Serves 4**

2 tbsp honey
4 pears (peeled & stalks on)
1 tsp cinnamon
1 tsp lemon juice
1 flan (ready-made)
4 ½ tbsp mascarpone
50 ml boiling water
Garnish:
Mint

Method

1. Put the lemon juice, boiling water, cinnamon, honey, ½ tbsp of mascarpone in a bowl and mix.
2. Add the peeled pears and gently coat with the mixture.
3. Set the hot air fryer to 170°c (if applicable). Pour into a suitable dish and place in a hot air fryer basket or directly into the hot air fryer pan, and cook for 8-10 minutes.

4. Cut a 5cm ring out of the flan, slice the ring into two discs (base & lid). Put the base in the ring and in the centre of the base place 1 tbsp of mascarpone and replace the lid and press down. (repeat for the other three pears)
5. Put on a plate, cut the bottom off the pear (so it will stand up) place on top of the flan and pour over the remaining mixture.

57

Top Tip!...Add crushed nuts instead of desiccated coconut.

Hot Pineapple with Chocolate

Ingredients   **Serves 4**

1 fresh pineapple
2 tbsp raisins
2 tbsp dark rum
1 tbsp brown sugar
1 tbsp desiccated coconut
6 cubes milk or dark chocolate (melted)

Method

1. Peel and core the pineapple and cut into four pieces.
2. Cut slices into the pineapple.
3. Fill the pineapple slices with rum, raisins and brown sugar.
4. Set the hot air fryer to 170°c (if applicable). Place two pineapple segments into a suitable dish and place in a Hot air fryer basket or directly into the hot air fryer pan, and cook for 8 minutes.

5. Repeat this process again to cook the remaining pineapple.
6. Serve on a plate, sprinkle with the coconut and drizzle with the melted chocolate.

Serve with ice cream.

Top Tip!... Instead of peaches, try using apricots or plums.

Peaches with Almonds

Ingredients   **Serves 4**

4 peaches
1 tbsp flaked almonds
2 tbsp almond liqueur
1 tbsp honey
1 tbsp dark brown sugar
2 tbsp mascarpone cheese
Garnish:
Mint

Method

1. Cut the peaches into quarters and remove the stones. Put into a bowl and mix with the flaked almonds, almond liqueur, honey and brown sugar.
2. Set the hot air fryer to 170°c (if applicable). Pour into a suitable dish and place in a hot air fryer basket or directly into the hot air fryer pan, and cook for 6-8 minutes.

Serve with a spoonful of mascarpone cheese.

Top Tip!... Various alternatives could be used, e.g. peach and raspberry, rhubarb, or plum and apple.

Upside Down Apple Crumble Desserts

Ingredients **Serves 4**

3 cooking apples
¼ tsp ground cinnamon
25g butter (melted)
50g brown sugar
50g sultanas
5 oat biscuits
440ml ready-made custard

Method

1. Peel, core and chop the apple into small pieces, place into a bowl and mix with brown sugar, sultanas, cinnamon and melted butter.
2. Set the hot air fryer to 170°c (if applicable). Pour into a suitable dish and place in a hot air fryer basket or directly into the hot air fryer pan, and cook for 6-10 minutes.
3. Crush the oat biscuits or chop in a food processor.
4. Layer the crushed oat biscuits, custard and apple in a dish and serve.

Serve with a cinnamon stick (optional).

Strawberry Flan

Ingredients　　　**Serves 6**

Topping
450g strawberries (1 punnet)
　　　(stalks removed)
2 tsp strawberry jam
1 tsp lemon juice
3 tbsp caster sugar
1 tbsp arrowroot mixed with 150ml
　　　cold water

Flan
1 readymade flan
4 tbsp Mascarpone
2 tbsp icing sugar
1 pint double cream
18 fresh strawberries (for base)
Oil for greasing

Method

1. Put the arrowroot, lemon juice, strawberries, strawberry jam, caster sugar in a bowl and mix.
2. Set the hot air fryer to 170°c (if applicable). Pour into a suitable dish and place in a Hot air fryer basket or directly into the hot air fryer pan, and cook for 12-15 minutes or until the sauce starts to go translucent.
3. Remove and leave to cool. Whip the double cream in a bowl, add the mascarpone and icing sugar and mix.
4. Cut a disc from the flan base using a 18cm food ring, then slice the ring into two pieces to form a base and lid.
5. Put the flan base into the food ring and grease the inside edge of the ring with a little oil.
6. Chop and halve the fresh strawberries and place around the edge of the food ring.
7. Fill the ring with the left over flan edges and mascarpone mix, then place the lid on the top.
8. Pour over the cooled strawberry mixture and garnish with a mint leaf and a dusting of icing sugar. Carefully remove food ring. ***Add a spun sugar nest topping (optional), see over. Recipe on page 66.***

65

To make spun sugar topping......

Warning !! Extreme caution should be taken with this dish as boiling sugar can burn and should be treated with respect. Take care when creating this dish.

1. Put 5 tbsp of caster sugar in a thick based, non-stick pan (not cast iron as it may crack and one where you do not care if it becomes damaged).
2. Place on a medium heat until golden brown, do not stir, but tilt from side-to-side to allow the sugars to fully dissolve.
3. Once it has turned into a golden brown liquid, remove the pan from the heat and place the bottom of the pan in cold water for 3 seconds, to stop the cooking process .
4. Protect floor coverings (or alternatively I go into the garden).Using a fork, scoop some of the mixture from the pan and wave carefully across a rolling pin or wooden spoon. Repeat this action to form the spun sugar. Ensure that you and other people are out of harm's way.
5. Take the spun sugar and form a nest. Place on top of the dessert. Use spun sugar immediately as it does not stay pliable for long. It can be reheated to soften.
6. For cleaning, place some water into the pan, return to the heat and simmer until all the sugar is dissolved within the liquid and then clean in hot soapy water as normal.